RAVEN

THE TOWN THAT NEVER WAS

An Illustrated Guide

Simon M. Rhodes

SMaRt Publications

Published by

SMaRt Publications

PO Box 146, Scarborough,
North Yorkshire, YO12 4YL

ISBN 0 9531033 1 5

First Edition Published August 1997
Second Edition Published April 1998

Cover illustration: The view from Raven Hall Road.

Authors Disclaimer

Whilst every care was taken in the preparation of this book, all routes are
undertaken at the individuals own risk. Neither the author nor the
publisher can accept any responsibility whatsoever for any consequences
arising out of using this book. Although the author encountered no
difficulty of access on the routes described, this does not imply that a
legal right of way or access exists.

INTRODUCTION

Y ou can't help but feel that Ravenscar has had a bit of a rough deal in the past. The village possesses one of, if not the finest views in Yorkshire looking northwest across the splendour of Robin Hoods Bay from its 600ft high vantage point. The village was intended to compete with the nearby towns of Scarborough and Whitby as a holiday resort in the late 19th century if the Victorian planners dreams had come true.

Today however, it exists as a mixture of buildings in different architectural styles dotted around in no particular form, like a giant hand had cast them to the land, as if sowing seed.

Ravenscar for many visitors means just a splendid view across Robin Hoods Bay that can be enjoyed without leaving the comfort of their car. But what a shame, because with a little effort a host of features can be discovered within a small area. So go forth, armed with this guide book of course, on a journey of discovery to the past, where you'll find the real Ravenscar - The Town That Never Was.

The National Trust now own the majority of the cliff top, where the proposed town was to be constructed and also the disused Peak Alum works and quarries.

Most of the other land is now privately owned and for this reason when exploring the area, please stay to the public rights of way and highways.

Oh, and one more thing. Should you decide to take mans best friend on your explorations, do keep him or her on a lead - this is sheep breeding country.

GEOLOGICAL ASPECTS

The geology at Ravenscar has played a major role in the way that man has over the centuries altered the visual aspect of the local landscape and to appreciate these changes more fully it's necessary to take a brief look at the geological formation.

The upland plateau of the North York Moors consists almost entirely of sedimentary rock (ie. compressed sediments on sea and river beds) laid down during the Jurassic period (213 million - 150 million years ago), and here on the coast at Ravenscar its many layers are exposed for all to see.

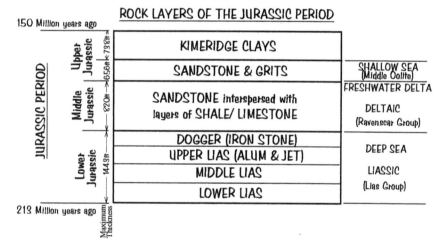

ROCK LAYERS OF THE JURASSIC PERIOD

150 Million years ago

JURASSIC PERIOD	Upper Jurassic	←65.0m→←73.8m→	KIMERIDGE CLAYS	
			SANDSTONE & GRITS	SHALLOW SEA (Middle Oolite)
	Middle Jurassic	62.0m	SANDSTONE interspersed with layers of SHALE/ LIMESTONE	FRESHWATER DELTA DELTAIC (Ravenscar Group)
	Lower Jurassic	144.9m	DOGGER (IRON STONE)	DEEP SEA
			UPPER LIAS (ALUM & JET)	LIASSIC (Lias Group)
			MIDDLE LIAS	
			LOWER LIAS	

213 Million years ago — Maximum Thickness

The Lias series of rock layers were created in the early Jurassic period from fine mud compressed on the floor of a deep sea and appear as a grey crumbly shale. They are rich in marine fossils such as Ammonites and belomites. It was from the upper lias shales that Alum was once extracted.

Above the Lias shale runs a 1 metre thick layer of Iron ore (Dogger) and above that several hundred feet of hard wearing sandstone (Deltaic series).

THE PEAK FAULT

About 35 million years ago, around the same time as the leg of Italy was colliding with mainland Europe to form the Alps, great forces were at work in this part of the world. Here the sedimentary rock layers buckled and folded under the immense pressure and at Ravenscar the layers fractured and moved sideways at a point now known as PEAK FAULT. This fracture created what appears to be a vertical displacement of several hundred feet between the rock layers on the northwestern side of the fault line and the same rock layers to the southeast of the line.

To the southeast of the fault, soft shales are exposed at sea level, while to the northwest the harder sandstone is found at sea level. This has created a situation where soft lias rock has eroded away to form bays along the coast heading north, while to the south the harder sandstone has produced a more uniform coast line.

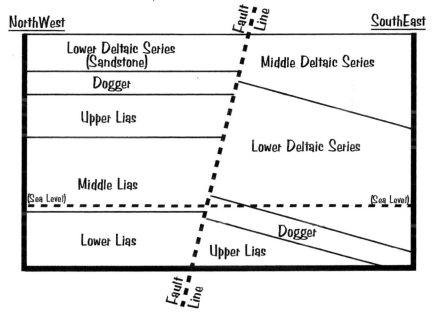

The exposure of Lias shale above sea level allowed the Alum industry to flourish, whilst the band of sandstone created an ample supply of building stone for the proposed town.

HISTORY OF THE LANDSCAPE

Apart from the presence of few Tumuli burial mounds on the higher land to the west, little is known of Ravenscar before Roman times. On the site where the Raven Hall Hotel now stands, evidence has been found to confirm that this was the location of a Roman signal station / fortlet in the form of an inscribed stone which workmen uncovered in 1774 while digging the foundations for Peak House, the forerunner of the now hotel. The stone, held in the Whitby museum, bears a Latin inscription of which the English translation is:

"Justinian, Governor of the Province and Vindician, General of the forces of upper Britain for the second time, with the younger provincial solders, made this fort, the manager of public works giving his assistance"

thereby making it probably the earliest known example of a YTS job! The Ravenscar signal station was one of five built on the east coast between the Tees estuary and Filey Brigg in about AD 367 to create a defensive system that could alert the inland armies of sea born attacks from Saxon raiders. The remains of the other stations are almost identical, so it appears reasonable to assume that the Ravenscar station was also of similar construction. The watch tower built of timber or stone was 50 feet square and 100 feet high, and situated within a massive outer wall 25 feet from the tower, with round corners and an outwards projecting tower at each corner. The whole site was enclosed by a ditch 30ft feet beyond the wall.

The Ravenscar fort was positioned in-between the stations at Scarborough and Goldsborough. ('Borough' referring to a Roman Castle). It is quite likely that a Roman road linked the Signal station to an inland fort, where help could be summoned, perhaps at Malton which would be almost in a direct line with the now named Raven Hall Road.

After the Romans had withdrawn from Britain in AD 407, the Angles arrived and moved inland to settle in the many valleys. Tun, the modern equivalent of which is ton meaning an enclosed farmstead or settlement is found in Stainton Dale the parish in which Ravenscar resides.

Could this dale to the south have been an area where the Angles settled and started farming in around AD 547? If so the woodland of the area may have been cleared for farming around this time.

Around AD 800, Danish Pirates are reputed to have landed here and climbing to the clifftop raised a flag on which was a motif containing the picture of a Raven, hence the origin of the place name. It's uncertain whether any locals actually witnessed this act. With a bunch of marauding pirates about to be let loose on the local countryside, I don't suppose many hung around to view the scene and so the actual origin of the story will remain unjustifiable - but it's a good story and gets my vote.

Moving into the Middle Ages, farming continued to be the main occupation in the area. The monks of Whitby abbey built a deer park at Fyling just north west of Ravenscar, with stone walls marking the boundary. Parts of the wall can still be seen today, with a stone cross embedded into the wall to identify the landowner.

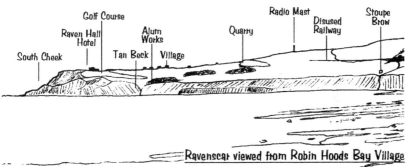

Ravenscar viewed from Robin Hoods Bay Village

It wasn't until 1640 when Alum was found in an exposure of the rocks by Sir Bryan Cooke that a dramatic change in the landscape occurred. A processing factory to extract the Alum from the Lias shales was built on the cliff top. A workforce of over 100 men started to cut away at the rock on the edge of the Moor, forming two large quarries with the waste dumped into large spoil heaps.

Alum was used extensively in the textile and tanning industries from the 1600's to the late 1800's as a fixer of dyes and to help make leather more supple. It also had its uses as early medical cures, for the treatment of chilblains, to help stop bleeding and even as an effective contraceptive!

When the price of Alum became high it was a much sought after product and it wasn't uncommon for raids from Dutch, French and Spanish pirates to take place. The Alum works at Low Peak (Peak was the former name of Ravenscar. The name change occurred in 1897) were defended by a

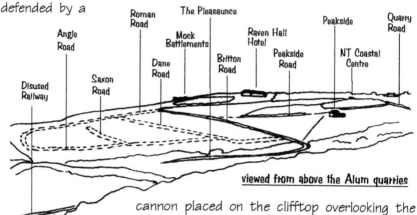

viewed from above the Alum quarries

cannon placed on the clifftop overlooking the small dock, where the ships would transport the finished product by sea. Billet Scar shown on the OS map is directly under the point where the cannon was located. Could "Billet", meaning the lodgings of a soldier, perhaps have something to do with the defending of the Alum works? Or a platoon of redcoats who were known to be stationed at the nearby Robin Hoods Bay to counter the smuggling?

When the demand for Alum started to fall due to the invention of synthetic dyes that did not require fixing, the industry went into decline, with the Peak works eventually closing in 1862.

The already mentioned Peak House (paragraph 1, come on keep up!) was built in 1774 for a Capt. Child of London, overlooking what was by now, quite an industrial landscape. Why anybody should have desired to build a house over looking an Alum works is quite beyond me, as one of the principle processes in the manufacture is to soak the shale in large vats containing urine. This essential ingredient was purchased and shipped in from as far away as London. In those days nobody put their milk bottles out on the door step at night empty! As Capt. Child sat on his front lawn, the smell of stale urine wafting on the evening breeze must have been delightful.

The house changed hands in the 1780's when it was acquired by the Rev. Francis Willis, who ran a private asylum in Lincolnshire. Willis treated King George III for his bouts of madness, having permission to use straitjackets, leaches and the occasional flogging on the King for medicinal purposes of course. It is reputed that the King used the house as a retreat in which to convalesce, but their is no evidence to support this. Willis erected a coat of arms in the grounds that bears the Royal coat of arms, but this was probably Willis been a little over optimistic.

When the King died in 1820, Willis billed the Royal court for £20,000 for his services. With the money he added mock battlements to the house using some stone from

ST. Hilda's Church

the now declining Alum works and from the old piers at Robin Hoods Bay. He also laid out formal garden in which he created Iron trees with metal leaves that would jingle in the wind. It is reputed that great parties were held at the house. As well as a great entertainer, Willis was also a gambler. In the 1840's he lost the entire house and grounds to a gentleman called W. H. Hammond in a single bet on a race between two wood lice across a saucer.

Hammond the new owner, was a business man and used the house as a holiday home as he lived most of the time in London. However in 1852 he built St Hilda's C of E Church at which his son and one of his daughters were married (though not to each other).

An amusing story in an 1965 edition of the Dalesman tells the tale that a man had to be shot so they could start a cemetery, as Ravenscar is supposedly one of the healthiest places in the country to live.

With the coming of the Railway to Ravenscar in 1884, came an additional problem. W. H. Hammond who was also the Chairman of the North Eastern Railway Company, insisted on having a 279 yard tunnel constructed under the now Raven Hall road, so that the line wouldn't spoil the view from his house. This unnecessary feature was duly done at an extra cost of £500. With only a thin layer of rock above, the tunnel was very wet inside, and combined with a sea fret and the 1:39 gradient, the steam engines would lose traction and slip to a standstill inside. Then a process of reversing down the track to the old alum quarries where they could build up steam and have another run at it would have to take place. This process would sometimes be repeated up to 5 times before the train could finally reach the station.

The tunnel was a short lived luxury for Hammond and when he died in 1895, the house and entire estate were sold for £10,000 to a development company calling themselves the Ravenscar Estate Company Ltd.

The new estate company set to work with 300 men laying drains, constructing roads and creating gardens in an attempt to create a new

Station Square shops

seaside resort that would challenge the likes of the already established ones, such as Scarborough and Whitby.

In a cunning piece of marketing to attract potential purchasers, the estate company decided that the name 'Peak' wasn't catchy enough for this trendy new resort and changed it to 'Ravenscar' on the 18th October 1897.

Building plots were offered for sale at auctions. With the promise of the train fare refunded if they should buy, special excursion trains were laid on to bring the potential purchasers from the cities of the West Riding and Midlands. Train fares in 1898 for 1st class return were from York 14' 0d, Malton 8' 6d, Market Weighton 15' 8d and Thirsk 16' 4d. Not much return against the price of a plot.

The estate company's sales brochure of 1900 tells of the many splendours of the site, such as the Terraces and Hanging Gardens at the Northern end of the Esplanade which could be entered via a turnstile at a charge of 2d per visitor. One lady visitor in the summer of 1896 exclaimed after admiring the view from the terraces across Robin Hoods Bay, "I feel like the Queen of Sheba after witnessing the splendours of Solomon". As far as a view goes it's good, but not that good! The hanging gardens below the terrace were reached by a zig zag path in the cliff face. At the end of this path was built a small turret on which was mounted an ancient gun said to have been around the world with Drake. The brochure tells of the Marine Esplanade, a mile long and laid out for detached residences upon the land side only, with the expanse of

The Avenue

meadow land between it and the cliff protected by a low wall forming the cliff park. In 1897 Peak House, now converted into a hotel was renamed the Raven Hall Hotel, and had an additional 50 accommodation rooms constructed.

The estate company's main selling points to its prospective clients, were the advantages that Ravenscar possessed, such as:

1. An ideal supply of pure water from moorland streams (However the two reservoirs that were built on the hillside to supply the town dried up!)

2. A face of building Stone in the quarries not less than 200ft in depth.

3. A bed of brick earth ten feet thick, a hill of building sand and a stratum of limestone in the face of the cliff.

4. The Railway line (North Eastern Railway Company) runs for a mile through the estate.

They then went on to say that:

"With these great natural advantages and with the huge population of the West Riding and Midlands behind it, annually overcrowding the existing outlets to the sea, it needs little prescience to foresee that the future of Ravenscar as a watering place is practically assured".

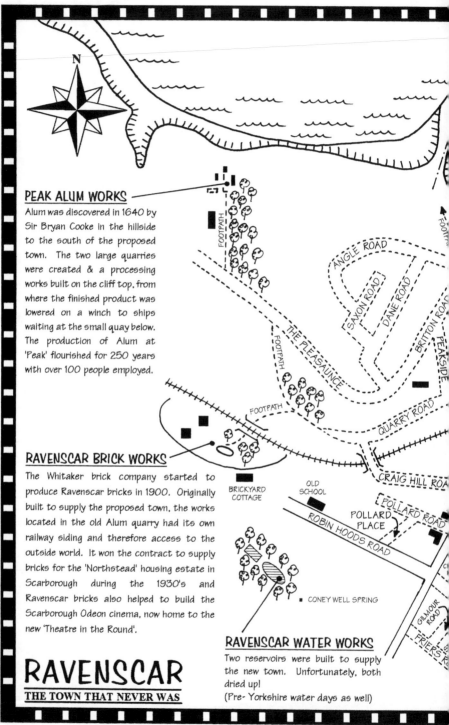

PEAK ALUM WORKS

Alum was discovered in 1640 by Sir Bryan Cooke in the hillside to the south of the proposed town. The two large quarries were created & a processing works built on the cliff top, from where the finished product was lowered on a winch to ships waiting at the small quay below. The production of Alum at 'Peak' flourished for 250 years with over 100 people employed.

RAVENSCAR BRICK WORKS

The Whitaker brick company started to produce Ravenscar bricks in 1900. Originally built to supply the proposed town, the works located in the old Alum quarry had its own railway siding and therefore access to the outside world. It won the contract to supply bricks for the 'Northstead' housing estate in Scarborough during the 1930's and Ravenscar bricks also helped to build the Scarborough Odeon cinema, now home to the new 'Theatre in the Round'.

RAVENSCAR
THE TOWN THAT NEVER WAS

RAVENSCAR WATER WORKS

Two reservoirs were built to supply the new town. Unfortunately, both dried up!
(Pre- Yorkshire water days as well)

Map labels: FOOTPATH, ANGLE ROAD, SAXON ROAD, DANE ROAD, BRITTON ROAD, PEAKSIDE, THE PLEASAUNCE, QUARRY ROAD, CRAIG HILL ROAD, POLLARD ROAD, POLLARD PLACE, ROBIN HOODS ROAD, OLD SCHOOL, BRICKYARD COTTAGE, CONEY WELL SPRING, GILMOUR ROAD, FRIERS

PEAK FAULT

The Peak fault occurred 35 million years ago, but was only discovered about 150 years ago. The fault has displaced the rock layers, so that to the east the Deltaic series (Sandstone) is at sea level, and to the west the Lias shales are at sea level. This is a displacement of 200 - 300ft and allowed man to extract the Alum from the Lias shales without drowning!

RAVENHALL HOTEL

Starting life as 'Peak House' in 1774, the hotel has been added to over the years. Once the home of Rev. Francis Willis who treated King George III for madness, it reputedly changed hands as a wager on a race between two wood lice across a saucer!

Bought by the Ravenscar Development Company in 1895, it was converted into a hotel and apart from a short spell as a military training establishment during W.W.II, has remained one ever since.

THE PROPOSED TOWN

The 'Ravenscar Estate Company' bought the entire area for £10,000 in 1895. In an attempt to create a new seaside resort, 300 men were employed to lay drains and construct new roads. Plots were offered for sale, but few buyers were tempted. The company went bust in 1913, with only a handful of houses built.

Map labels:
INDER CLIFF
SHELTER
SHELTER
SHELTER
SHELTER
HAMMOND ROAD
WILLIS ROAD
THE CRESCENT
MARINE ESPLANADE
STATION ROAD
HAMMOND ROAD
DERWENT STREET
ARNOLD ROAD
ST HILDA'S ROAD
LORING ROAD
CHURCH ROAD
LDAS RCH
VILLAGE HALL
HILLCREST
BENT RIGG LANE
STATION SQUARE
DISUSED RAILWAY TRACK

This statement couldn't have been further from the truth. Unlike the Romans who went before them, the good people of the West Riding and Midlands came, they saw, and they went home again - not surprisingly without buying. With a 400ft drop to the beach, and exposure to the north easterly gales that blew away the shelters on the Marine esplanade its no wonder that the public didn't buy, and in 1913 the company went into liquidation, although some sources allege it to still have a registered office in London.

Another business venture which one would think would also have been doomed from the start, was the creation of the Whitaker brick works that came into operation in 1900 on the site of the old alum quarry. Built mainly to supply the proposed housing development, the owners had the foresight to have their own railway siding and therefore the ability to supply their bricks over a wide area. The Ravenscar brick works won the contract to supply bricks for the 'Northstead' housing estate in Scarborough during the 1920's much to the surprise of their competitors, the Scarborough brick company. Ravenscar bricks also helped to build the Scarborough Odeon cinema in the 1930's. The two brick works chimneys of 60ft and 100ft were finally demolished in 1960.

The shelters on the Marine Esplanade weren't the only articles to suffer from the bad weather at Ravenscar. In 1947, the railway line was blocked for six weeks with snow drifts in the cuttings of up to 12ft. It is said that the snow was almost level with the signals at Ravenscar station. With the closure of the railway in 1965, as part of the Beeching cuts, the area is slowly losing its urban appearance. From the industrial landscape of the Alum production through the urbanisation of the proposed town, the area is once more reverting back to a rural landscape.

In the 1970's the remains of the former Peak alum works, the brick works and the clifftop area of the 'Town That Never Was', were acquired by the National Trust.

The Mock Battlements

EXPLORING THE PROPOSED TOWN

This exploration of the proposed town is divided into two halves. One easy. One not so easy! It can be tailored to suit your own requirements depending on how fit/unfit, lazy or pushed for time you are!

WALK ONE - 1 Hour (Distance - 1½ miles) →-→-- →-

The first half covers the area of roads on the cliff top (now owned by the National Trust) the layout of which are still visible. Station Square, Loring Road and returning to the National Trust Coastal Centre. The whole of this walk is on the level.

WALK TWO - 1½ Hours (Distance - 2 miles) →• • →••

The second half covers the old brick works, an optional detour to view the remains of the Alum works and the road layout now covered by the Hotels golf course. This walk is more physically demanding with a good pull back up to the finish.

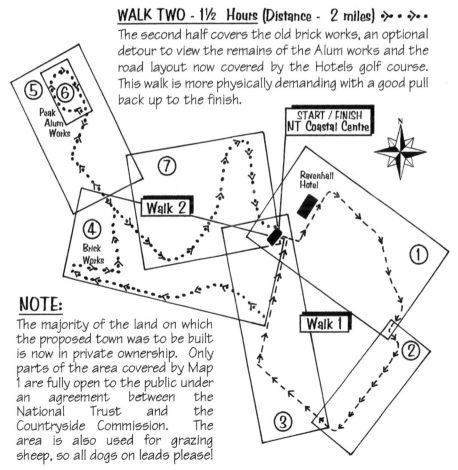

NOTE:

The majority of the land on which the proposed town was to be built is now in private ownership. Only parts of the area covered by Map 1 are fully open to the public under an agreement between the National Trust and the Countryside Commission. The area is also used for grazing sheep, so all dogs on leads please!

RAVENSCAR
THE TOWN THAT NEVER WAS

MAP 1	HAMMOND ROAD & MARINE ESPLANADE

WALK ONE	Time: 1 Hour	Distance: 1½ Miles

① Leave the NT Coastal Centre onto Station Road. After 100 metres turn left into Hammond Road, signposted 'Cleveland Way'

The drainage covers and kerbing stones are clearly visible heading towards the cliff top.

② Continue to the end of the road, passing the junctions of 'The Crescent' and the 'Marine Esplanade' on the right.

On reaching the cliff top, a circular concrete base can be seen. This is all that remains of one of the shelters that blew away during a gale in the early 1900's. Turning to your right the area between the cliff top and the Marine Esplanade was once laid out as the cliff park surrounded by a low wall.

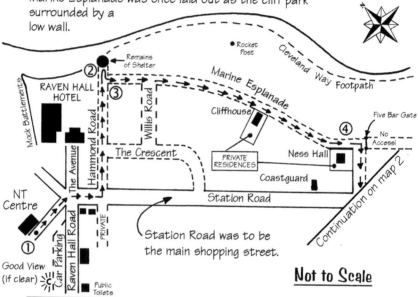

Station Road was to be the main shopping street.

Not to Scale

③ Retrace your steps before following the Marine Esplanade, passing 'Cliffhouse' and 'Ness Hall'. (Both these houses are in private ownership so please respect their privacy).

This is where your imagination has to be let loose. Try to imagine a whole street of houses like 'Cliffhouse' and you get a picture of how the Esplanade could have appeared. At the field gate in front of you the continuing line of the Esplanade is still visible although now grassed over.

④ Turn right, crossing Station Road and into Station Square.

MAP 2 | STATION SQUARE & LORING ROAD

To the left is a red brick building, once the Station Master's house. Directly ahead are a flight of steps leading onto the Station platform which is now overgrown.

5 Either go up the steps, turn left and walk along the platform or turn left at the bottom of the steps following the sign for 'Loring Road'. Turn right and cross the old level crossing in to the wide and unsurfaced 'Loring Road'.

On the left are examples of the type of buildings that may have lined the entire road if circumstances had been different. Once again it's time to let your imagination take over!

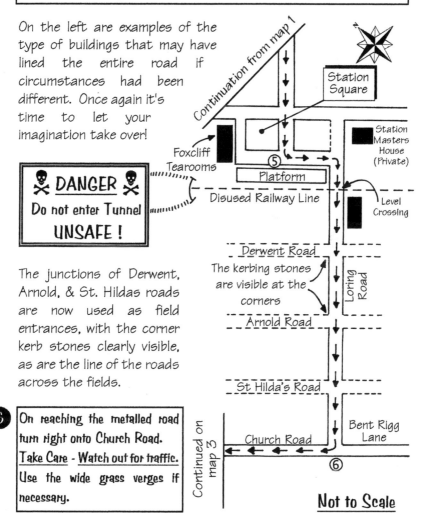

☠ DANGER ☠

Do not enter Tunnel

UNSAFE !

The junctions of Derwent, Arnold, & St. Hildas roads are now used as field entrances, with the corner kerb stones clearly visible, as are the line of the roads across the fields.

6 On reaching the metalled road turn right onto Church Road. Take Care - Watch out for traffic. Use the wide grass verges if necessary.

Not to Scale

RAVENSCAR
THE TOWN THAT NEVER WAS

MAP 3	CHURCH ROAD & CRAIG HILL ROAD

THE MIDWAY POINT or the finish for those whose legs refuse to go any further!

7 | Continue along Church Road until the T-Junction

Just after Hillcrest (White bungalow) on the left the first old road can be observed - now used as a farm track.

Just before the cricket pavilion, an entrance shows the once line of Gilmour road.

On reaching the T-juction, 'Pollard Road' (straight ahead) now leads into a farm yard (Private). ST. Hilda's church on the corner, was built in 1852 by W. H. Hammond who owned the Raven Hall.

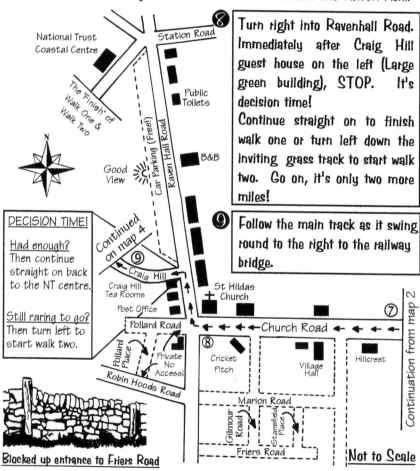

8 Turn right into Ravenhall Road. Immediately after Craig Hill guest house on the left (Large green building), STOP. It's decision time!
Continue straight on to finish walk one or turn left down the inviting grass track to start walk two. Go on, it's only two more miles!

9 Follow the main track as it swing round to the right to the railway bridge.

National Trust Coastal Centre

Station Road

Public Toilets

The 'Finish' of Walk One & Walk Two

N

Car Parking (Free)

Raven Hall Road

B&B

Good View

DECISION TIME!
Had enough? Then continue straight on back to the NT centre.

Still raring to go? Then turn left to start walk two.

Continued on map 4

9

Craig Hill

Craig Hill Tea Rooms

Post Office

Pollard Road

Pollard Place

Private No Access!

Robin Hoods Road

St Hildas Church

Church Road

7

8

Cricket Pitch

Village Hall

Hillcrest

Marion Road

Gilmour Road

Stansfield Place

Friers Road

Continuation from map 2

Not to Scale

Blocked up entrance to Friers Road

Page 18

MAP 4 | THE OLD BRICK WORKS & THE PLEASAUNCE

WALK TWO - THE START

❶ On reaching the railway bridge, descend to the railway track via the steps on the left. At the bottom turn left and continue until you pass over a stone bridge by a wooden seat.

This is the bed of the old Scarborough to Whitby railway, closed in 1965 as part of the Beeching cuts. You are now walking downhill on a gradient of 1:39, although it doesn't seem like it at times!

DECISION TIME ONCE AGAIN!

Turn left here to detour and view the remains of the Peak Alum works.
OR turn right to continue the walk bypassing the Alum works.

❷ Turn left into the disused quarry. Surrounded by a wire fence are the remains of the brick works kilns.

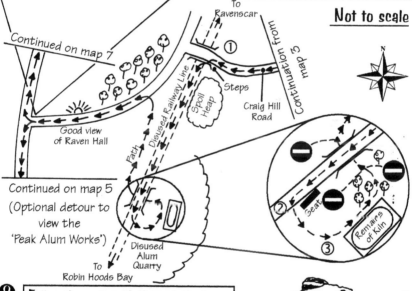

Not to scale

To Ravenscar

Continued on map 7

Good view of Raven Hall

Continued on map 5 (Optional detour to view the 'Peak Alum Works')

To Robin Hoods Bay

Steps

Craig Hill Road

Continuation from map 3

Disused Railway Line

Spoil Heap

Path

Disused Alum Quarry

Seat

Remains of Kiln

❸ Follow the main path through the trees, and under the railway bridge. The path swings to the right and runs parallel with the railway line until it joins a wide track. Turn left and head downhill to the next junction.

The remains of part of the Kiln on the site of the old Whitaker brickworks

MAP 5 | THE PEAK ALUM WORKS (OPTIONAL DETOUR)

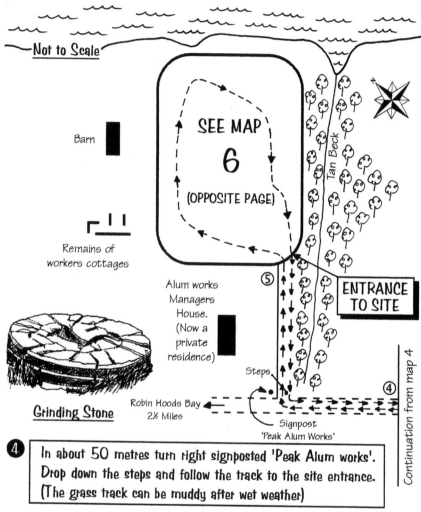

Not to Scale

Barn

SEE MAP
6
(OPPOSITE PAGE)

Tan Beck

Remains of
workers cottages

Alum works
Managers
House.
(Now a
private
residence)

⑤

ENTRANCE
TO SITE

Steps

④

Continuation from map 4

Grinding Stone

Robin Hoods Bay
2½ Miles

Signpost
'Peak Alum Works'

④ In about 50 metres turn right signposted 'Peak Alum works'. Drop down the steps and follow the track to the site entrance. (The grass track can be muddy after wet weather)

The Peak Alum works were acquired by the National Trust in 1979 under the Enterprise Neptune Appeal. Work on restoring the site started in 1984 and now contains some of the most extensive Alum work remains in Yorkshire.

⑤ On leaving the site, simply retrace your steps. Continue onto Map 4.

MAP 6 | The Peak Alum Works

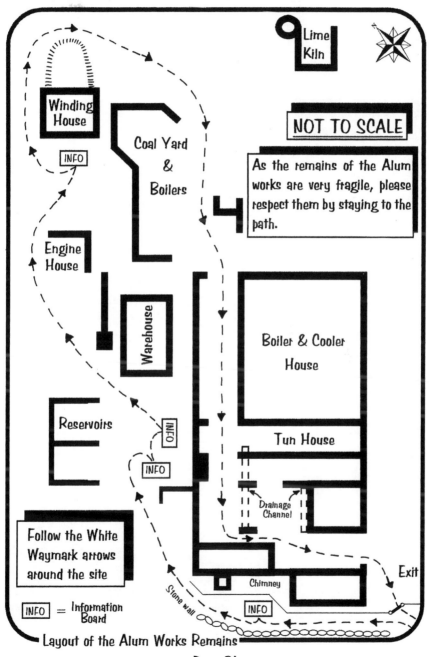

Lime Kiln

NOT TO SCALE

As the remains of the Alum works are very fragile, please respect them by staying to the path.

Winding House

INFO

Coal Yard & Boilers

Engine House

Warehouse

Boiler & Cooler House

Reservoirs

INFO

INFO

Tun House

Drainage Channel

Follow the White Waymark arrows around the site

Stone wall

Chimney

Exit

INFO

INFO = Information Board

Layout of the Alum Works Remains

MAP 7 | BRITTON ROAD & ROMAN ROAD

6 Follow the Pleasaunce, crossing over two cattle grids. After crossing the second grid the Golf course is entered.

To the left the raised outline of Dane Road can be seen as it crosses one of the greens.

7 Continue along Britton Road, around to the right and climb up Roman road as it runs parallel to the Mock Battlements. At the top, turn right back to the National Trust Coastal Centre and the finish.

Time now for the obligatory end of walk cuppa and sticky bun!

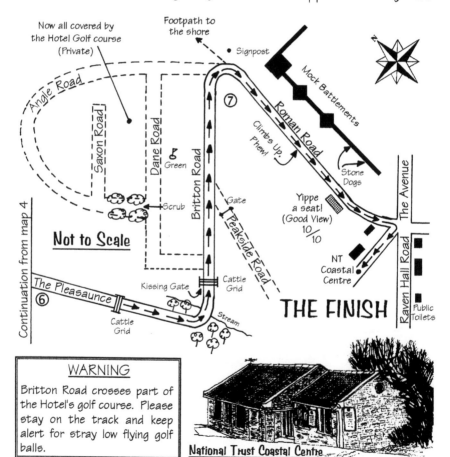

Now all covered by the Hotel Golf course (Private)

Footpath to the shore

Signpost

Mock Battlements

Angle Road

Saxon Road

Dane Road

Green

Britton Road

Roman Road

Climbs Up. Phew!

Stone Dogs

The Avenue

Scrub

Gate

Yippe a seat! (Good View) 10/10

Not to Scale

Peakside Road

NT Coastal Centre

Raven Hall Road

Continuation from map 4

The Pleasaunce

6

Kissing Gate

Cattle Grid

Stream

Cattle Grid

THE FINISH

Public Toilets

WARNING

Britton Road crosses part of the Hotel's golf course. Please stay on the track and keep alert for stray low flying golf balls.

National Trust Coastal Centre

CHRONOLOGY

300AD   Roman Signal station / Fort constructed and occupied.

800AD   Danes landed and raised a flag bearing an emblem containing a Raven.

1640   Sir Bryan Cooke discovered Alum at Peak.

1774   Peak House built for Capt. Child of London. (Inscribed foundation stone of the Roman signal station discovered, now in Whitby Museum).

1788   Rev. Francis Willis started to treat King George III and obtains Peak House.

1820   King George III died. Willis billed Royal court £20,000 for his services. Used the money to lay out gardens and add mock battlements.

1840's   Rev. Willis loses Peak House to W.H. Hammond in a wager between two wood lice running across a saucer.

1852   W.H. Hammond built St. Hildas church.

1884   Railway Completed. (A 279 yard tunnel built under Raven Hall Road at an extra cost of £500, so as not to spoil the view from the Hall.)

1895   W.H. Hammond dies and the Hall and estate are sold for £10,000 to a development company. (Ravenscar Estate Company Ltd.)

1897   (18th October) Name changed from Peak to Ravenscar and work on the proposed housing estate started.

1898   Raven Hall purchased by the Hudson Hotels Ltd.

1900   Whitakers Brickwork's opened on the site of the old Alum quarry.

1913   Ravenscar estate company went bust.

1920   Ravenhall Hotel sold.

1934   Heated outdoor swimming pool added to the hotel.

1939   Ravenhall Hotel used as a military training establishment during W.W.II.

1947   Ravenscar snowed in for six weeks with 12ft of snow.

1960   Ravenhall Hotel sold to the present owners.

1960   The two Brickwork's chimneys (60ft and 100ft) were demolished.

1965   Railway closed as part of the Beeching cuts.

1970's   Peak Alum works site, the Alum quarry and the clifftop area of the proposed town acquired by the National Trust.

BIBLIOGRAPHY

Anon, 1965, Dalesman, The Dalesman Publishing Company Ltd, Lancaster.

Carstairs I, 1987, The North York Moors National Park - Countryside Commission Official Guide, Webb & Bower (Publishers) Ltd, Exeter.

Hoskins W. G., 1955,The Making of the English Landscape, Penguin Books Ltd, London.

North York Moors National Park Information Service, 1981, Ravenscar Geological Trail, North Moors National Park, Helmsley.

North Yorkshire & Cleveland Heritage Coast, 1989, Heritage Coast Geology, North York Moors National Park Information service, Helmsley.

North York Moors Information Service, Year unknown, Peak Alum Works - Ravenscar, North York Moors National Park, Helmsley.

Rackham O., 1986, The History of the Countryside, J.M. Dent & Sons Ltd, London.

Raistrick A., 1966, North York Moors - National Park Guide No. 4, Her Majesty's Stationery Office, London.

Ravenscar Estate Company Ltd, 1900, Ravenscar Sales Brochure.

Staniforth, A., 1990, Geology of the North York Moors, North York Moors National Park, Helmsley